Feeling Wrong in Your Own Body: Understanding What It Means to Be Transgender

The Gallup's Guide to Modern Gay, Lesbian, & Transgender Lifestyle

Feeling Wrong in Your Own Body: Understanding What it Means to Be Transgender

by Jaime A. Seba

Mason Crest Publishers

MASON CREST PUBLISHERS INC.
370 Reed Road
Broomall, Pennsylvania 19008
(866)MCP-BOOK (toll free)
www.masoncrest.com

First Printing
9 8 7 6 5 4 3 2 1

              Library of Congress Cataloging-in-Publication Data
Seba, Jaime.
 Feeling wrong in your own body : understanding what it means to be transgender / by Jaime A. Seba.
     p. cm.
 Includes bibliographical references and index.
 ISBN 978-1-4222-1746-7 (hbk.)   ISBN 978-1-4222-1758-0 (series)
 ISBN 978-1-4222-1866-2 (pbk.)   ISBN 978-1-4222-1863-1 (series pbk.)
 1. Transgenderism—Juvenile literature. 2. Transgender people—Identity—Juvenile literature. 3. Gender identity—Juvenile literature. I. Title.
 HQ77.9.S43 2011
 306.76'8—dc22
                         2010026822

Produced by Harding House Publishing Service, Inc.
www.hardinghousepages.com
Interior design by MK Bassett-Harvey.
Cover design by Torque Advertising + Design.
Printed in the USA by Bang Printing

PICTURE CREDITS

Achels, Fotolia: p.34
Arcady, Fotolia: p. 37
Arcurs, Yuri; Fotolia: p. 16
Blanchette, Leo; Fotolia: p. 10
Creative Commons: p. 45, 50, 54, 58
Fox Searchlight: p. 46

Oikawa, Kenji-Baptiste; Creative Commons: p. 27
PR Photos: p. 60
Struthers, Karen; Fotolia: p. 28
TransActive: p. 41
Zdorov, Kirill; Fotolia: p. 20
Zooropa, Fotolia: p. 24

Contents

Introduction

We are both individuals and community members. Our differences define individuality; our commonalities create a community. Some differences, like the ability to run swiftly or to speak confidently, can make an individual stand out in a way that is viewed as beneficial by a community, while the group may frown upon others. Some of those differences may be difficult to hide (like skin color or physical disability), while others can be hidden (like religious views or sexual orientation). Moreover, what some communities or cultures deem as desirable differences, like thinness, is a negative quality in other contemporary communities. This is certainly the case with sexual orientation and gender identity, as explained in *Homosexuality Around the World*, one of the volumes in this book series.

Often, there is a tension between the individual (individual rights) and the community (common good). This is easily visible in everyday matters like the right to own land versus the common good of building roads. These cases sometimes result in community controversy and often are adjudicated by the courts.

An even more basic right than property ownership, however, is one's gender and sexuality. Does the right of gender expression trump the concerns and fears of a community or a family or a school? *Feeling Wrong in Your Own Body*, as the author of that volume suggests, means confronting, in the most personal way, the tension between individuality and community. And, while a community, family, and school have the right (and obligation) to protect its children, does the notion of property rights extend to controlling young adults' choice as to how they express themselves in terms of gender or sexuality?

Changes in how a community (or a majority of the community) thinks about an individual right or responsibility often precedes changes in the law enacted by legislatures or decided by courts. And for these changes to occur, individuals (sometimes working in small groups) often defied popular opinion, political pressure, or religious beliefs. Some of these trends are discussed in *A New Generation of Homosexuality*. Every generation (including yours!) stands on the accomplishments of our ancestors and in *Gay and Lesbian Role Models* you'll be reading about some of them.

One of the most pernicious aspects of discrimination on the basis of sexual orientation is that "homosexuality" is a stigma that can be hidden (see the volume about *Homophobia*). While some of my generation (I was your age in the early 1960s) think that life is so much easier being "queer" in the age of the Internet, Gay-Straight Alliances, and Ellen, in reality, being different in areas where difference matters is *always* difficult. Coming Out, as described in the volume of the same title, is always challenging—for both those who choose to come out and for the friends and family they trust with what was once a hidden truth. Being healthy means being honest—at least to yourself. Having supportive friends and family is most important, as explained in *Being Gay, Staying Healthy*.

Sometimes we create our own "families"—persons bound together by love and identity but not by name or bloodline. This is quite common in gay communities today as it was several generations ago. Forming families or small communities based on rejection by the larger community can also be a double-edged sword. While these can be positive, they may also turn into prisons of conformity. Does being lesbian, for example, mean everyone has short hair, hates men, and drives (or rides on) a motorcycle? *What Does It Mean to Be Gay, Lesbian, Bisexual, or Transgender?* "smashes" these and other stereotypes.

Another common misconception is that "all gay people are alike"—a classic example of a stereotypical statement. We may be drawn together because of a common prejudice or oppression, but we should not forfeit our individuality for the sake of the safety of a common identity, which is one of the challenges shown in *Gay People of Color: Facing Prejudices, Forging Identities.*

Coming out to who *you* are is just as important as having a group or "family" within which to safely come out. Becoming knowledgeable about these issues (through the books in this series and the other resources to which they will lead), feeling good about yourself, behaving safely, actively listening to others *and* to your inner spirit—all this will allow you to fulfill your promise and potential.

James T. Sears, PhD
Consultant

chapter 1

What Is Gender?

Gender seems like a very simple idea. People accept that individuals are either male or female, and that's the end of it. But for those born into a body that doesn't feel right, it can be much more complicated.

Humans are generally divided into the male or female sex, which is distinguished by reproductive functions. Most people are born with **anatomical** differences that make them either male or female. Based on their sex, people have a specific gender identity. Someone who is born with a male anatomy usually has the gender identity of a boy, while those born with female anatomy have the gender identity of a girl.

But defining what it means to be a boy or a girl isn't as simple as biology. It is often dictated by our culture or society. For centuries, this

What's That Mean?

Anatomical has to do with the biological structure of the human body.

We can tell immediately by looking at the clothing and hairstyle of these drawings which is a boy and which is a girl. Pink for girls, blue for boys, and longer hair for girls are all gender characteristics our culture has assigned to the biological sexes.

nursery rhyme has reflected how most people think of the different genders:

What are little boys made of?
Frogs and snails and puppy dogs' tails,
That's what little boys are made of.

What are little girls made of?
Sugar and spice and all things nice,
That's what little girls are made of.

This rhyme, which many children learn when they are very small, defines boys as being rough and playing in the dirt with animals. In a similar way, boys are often given toys such as guns, soldiers, and cars. These are all considered to be masculine things. The poem depicts girls as being sweet and more fragile. Girls play with baby dolls and stuffed animals. Even clothing is designed to reflect gender roles. Men wear pants, suits, and ties, while women ***traditionally*** wore skirts and dresses with flowers and lace. Girls are pink. Boys are blue.

As they grow up, these messages continue. The traditional image is that boys play football, go to war,

What's That Mean?

Traditionally has to do with the accepted way things have been done over a long period of time.

become mechanics, and protect the home and family. Girls are cheerleaders, become nurses, and focus their lives on being wives and mothers.

But these accepted standards are not biological. There is nothing about an individual's sex that requires these corresponding gender roles. Women are not required to love flowers and lace simply

Examples of Sex Characteristics

- Women menstruate while men do not.
- Men have testicles while women do not.
- Women have developed breasts that can produce milk for babies, while men have not.
- Men generally have heavier bones than women.

Examples of Gender Characteristics

- In the United States (and most other countries), women earn significantly less money than men for similar work.
- In much of the Western world, women can wear dresses while men do not.
- In Saudi Arabia men are allowed to drive cars while women are not.
- In most of the world, women do more housework than men.

because they are biologically female. And in modern times, people are beginning to break away from traditional gender roles. As part of this change, some people find themselves questioning the gender role with which they are born. This is referred to as gender nonconforming—refusing to follow those traditionally accepted gender roles.

"While gender identities are internal to a person, gender roles are handed to us by society," said Dr. Laura Erickson-Schroth, who studies transgender health issues. "We should be teaching our children that whatever bodies they live in, they can choose to reject gender roles. For some gender-nonconforming people, it feels right to live in the bodies into which they are born, but to challenge gender-*normative* behaviors."

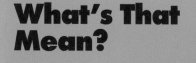

What's That Mean?

Behavior that is *normative* is considered normal and acceptable.

This is becoming increasingly more accepted, especially for women. Women fight in the armed forces and can have any career they choose. Young girls who play with boys or wear overalls are called "tomboys," and are barely given a second thought. In high school across America, girls are given as many options for sports and activities as boys. Women wear pants, suits, and even ties.

But it's not really the same for men.

"We live in a time when women can do anything they want," said Carolyn Gierga, a single woman in her thirties who owns her own home and has a thriving career in the medical field. "But it's still different for men. They're expected to be the ones who can fix things. They're expected to be strong and stable. Women do things that men do, and it's perfectly normal. But when men do things that women traditionally do, we think it's weird. Or we assume they're gay!"

For gender-nonconforming people, especially men, these traditional roles and rules of society can be very confusing. If a young boy enjoys singing and dancing, or even wearing dresses, it's immediately assumed that he's gay. But gender roles aren't necessarily related to sexuality. Just as little girls who are tomboys often grow up to be straight women, little boys who enjoy activities typically done by girls can still grow up to be straight men.

EXTRA INFO

Some sociologists are concerned that feminine gender qualities are still being looked down upon in our culture. They point out that the reason it's okay for women to dress and act like men, but not okay for men to dress and act like women, is because masculine behaviors are seen as strong, competent, professional, and admirable. So-called feminine qualities, however—being nurturing, sensitive, and creative—are looked upon as weaker, less admirable ways of being. Women may not face the same kinds of discrimination they once did, but only if they can conform to masculine gender roles, while men who want to push past the boundaries of those same gender roles *do* face discrimination. In other words, sex may no longer be the basis for prejudice and discrimination—but gender still is.

Notice how similarly these male and female businesspeople are dressed. Appropriate clothing for businesswomen is very much the same as men's clothing, with the implication being that if women can act like men, then they will be respected in the business world. Imagine if instead, the men were wearing attractive frilly dresses! The thought of a man dressed in feminine clothing seems silly and laughable, while a woman dressed in masculine clothing does not.

Researchers Madeline Heilman and Aaron Wallen from New York University and Columbia University, respectively, found that when men succeed in occupations traditionally held by women, the men are considered "wimpy" by their co-workers, and they are often treated with less respect. On the other hand, though, this is not the case for women who succeed in jobs usually held by men.

"So many people assume that **effeminate** men are always gay, and that does a disservice to both gay men and straight men, because it's so limiting," said Helena Barrett, who worked with a transgender advocacy group in Western New York. "Men, much more than women, are told they have to behave a certain way in order to be considered a 'real man.' When you really stop and think about that, it makes no sense at all. And I think it's encouraging that more and more, people are starting to think about those things. And they realize that we're all a lot happier if we can just be who we are."

Still, from the time people are born, they are often placed into the specific roles defined by their sex. This is called a gender **binary** system, meaning

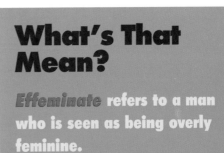

What's That Mean?

Effeminate refers to a man who is seen as being overly feminine.

A **binary** system is made up of two, and only two, parts.

that there are just two options for gender—male or female. Anyone who falls outside the traditional roles is considered weird or strange.

"*Ambiguity* has never been popular," said Rachel Kahn, a student at Bryn Mawr College who researched binary gender systems in sports. "We like to *categorize*, and we don't like it when people do not fit neatly into our categories."

Gender is the collection of behaviors and traits that society typically assigns to each sex. Gender roles change when society changes how it regards men and women. For centuries, society considered women to be less than men in many ways. But as culture progressed, women achieved basic equalities like the right to vote, and eventually reached their modern standing.

What's That Mean?

Ambiguity **means unclear and confusing.**

To *categorize* **is to mentally sort things into different groups.**

"If you look back in history books at the changes that have occurred in our society in the last hundred years, even, there have been so many ways that the roles of men and women have changed and expanded," Barrett said. "It just stands to reason that things will change just as much, if not more, in the next hundred years. It's arrogant for us to think that the way we look at things now is the only way they will ever

EXTRA INFO

For many parents today, the surprise of finding out if their child is male or female comes earlier than birth, due to the increased use of ultrasound machines. Although initially used to detect problems prenatally, the use of this technology is now almost routine. Ultrasound images can still help detect development problems, but they are also used to measure the fetus and let the parents know whether they'll be having a boy or girl. Once parents, friends, and family members know the child's sex, clothing and toys are purchased, many with a specific gender bias. Even the decorating of the nursery and certainly the selection of potential names can be influenced by the newborn's sex. The stage is set for the development of gender identity in the child.

Within each culture, and even each family unit, preconceived ideas exist about what it means to be male or female. As soon as the baby is born, the individuals with whom the child has contact will treat it as they believe a child of that particular sex should be treated. Parents tend to cuddle and hold female children more than males. Assertive play is often encouraged in male children. In most cases, but not all, that treatment will be based on the physical sex of the child.

be. We are constantly moving forward, constantly progressing."

Barrett was raised in a strict religion that adhered to very traditional gender roles. She always wore

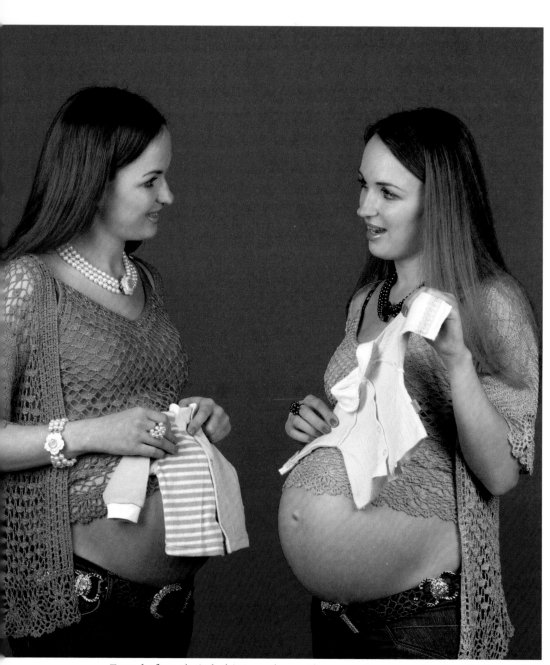

Even before their babies are born, these mothers are shaping their gender identities by choosing pink clothes for girl babies, blue for boy babies.

20   Feeling Wrong in Your Own Body

skirts, and her mother ingrained in her that "the purpose of life is to get married and have children." She wasn't encouraged to go to college or leave her parents' house until she was married and ready to live with a husband.

"I don't think there's anything wrong with behaving that way, but only if that's what someone actually wants," she said. "The problem is that it starts so early, when we're just little kids. We don't know enough to know who we really are yet. So all we can do is follow what people around us say and do, no matter whether or not it actually fits who we are. Would I have worn skirts every day if I had my own choice? I don't know. All I know is that I don't wear them now. Ever. And I know I'm still a woman."

FIND OUT MORE ON THE INTERNET

Changing Gender Roles
workingmoms.about.com/od/workingmomsresearch/a/
GenderRoles.htm

Gender Spectrum
www.genderspectrum.org

Gender Stereotypes
www.campbell-kibler.com/Stereo.pdf

READ MORE ABOUT IT

Abate, Michelle Ann. *Tomboys: A Literary and Cultural History.* Philadelphia, Penn.: Temple University Press, 2008.

Tyre, Peg. *The Trouble With Boys.* New York: Random House, 2008.

chapter 2

What Is Transgender?

Crossdresser, transsexual, intersex, gender-queer, drag queen, drag king, transgender—there are many terms used to describe people who dress, behave, or live as the opposite gender. These individuals are often referred to as transgender.

"Terminology can be intimidating when you're first learning about anything, and terminology surrounding identities of any kind—racial, sexual, etc.—can be even harder because it changes so rapidly," said Dr. Laura Erickson-Schroth, who answered questions on transgender issues for readers of *The New York Times* in 2010. "Even at a given point in time, people within certain groups will disagree about the meaning of terms. Young people have started to shorten the word 'transgender' to just 'trans,' and this shortened form can mean different things to different people."

Alex Yates, co-president of an **LGBT** activism group at Penn State University, led a student group discussion about gender issues. Part of the conversation was aimed at helping people understand the terms that can become confusing, especially for people who do not know any transgender individuals. Many questions arose about the correct terms to use for people who don't conform to traditional gender roles. He summarized the terminology as easily as possible.

"'Transgender' is an umbrella term for any gender-**variant** person," he said.

Being gender-variant means that the way a person thinks his or her gender doesn't match what society generally believes each gender to be. This may be a strong, masculine woman who fixes cars and wears ties or an effeminate man who enjoys arranging flowers. It may also be someone who doesn't identify with either gender entirely or even at all. Gender-variant may also refer to someone who goes through a surgical change to become a different sex. Some people also refer to gender variance as being "genderqueer."

"Some people identify as genderqueer because their gender identity is androgynous," said Erickson-Schroth. "Some use the term bi-gendered to describe themselves. Others identify as nongendered. Some people use the term genderqueer because they oppose the binary gender system."

She recommends the Transsexual Roadmap, an online resource of information for transgender issues that explains how different people approach the binary gender system of being either male or female. But in general, she explains that "transsexual" is an older term that has often been used for individuals who may have had a surgical procedure, but even if they have not, they still live as a different sex from what they were born. This is now frequently replaced with the term "transgender."

"There is a whole *spectrum* of transgender peo-

Gender is not a black-and-white quality, but rather it exists in a rainbow spectrum of variations and shadings.

ple, who live their lives in a variety of ways, and that makes it very difficult to define," said Helena Barrett, who led support groups for friends and families of transgender people. "They even have a hard time understanding themselves. People immediately recognize when they don't fit in with everyone else, but that doesn't mean they can figure out how to fix it or find where they *do* fit. It takes time and understanding.

"But when people have the opportunity to learn about their gender identity, and to explore who they really are, they can find what works best for them. There are many

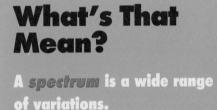

What's That Mean?

A *spectrum* is a wide range of variations.

ways that families and friends can support that. And the more research that is done, the more people can get the help they need to understand their own gender identity. The health industry has really been moving forward to find ways of supporting transgender people and providing the services that are needed."

The process of physically transitioning can take years. Hormone treatments, psychological counseling and evaluation, and surgery are only a few parts of the complex medical process.

In medical and other online resources, transgender is often noted as TG and transsexual as TS. Male to female (MTF) is used to describe someone who is born male, but who identifies as female. Female to male (FTM) is someone who is born female, but who identifies as male. Some prefer the term "trans man" (FTM) or "trans woman" (MTF). And a growing number of mental health professionals, like Erickson-Schroth, are doing research to gain a better understanding into the factors that contribute to issues of gender identity.

"I don't consider being transgender to be a mental health problem itself," Barrett said. "But, just like everyone else, I think transgender people can benefit from working with a mental health professional to understand and deal with their emotions and the pressures and stress that can come from resolving gender identity issues."

In addition to being transgender, some people

This trans woman was born male but identifies as female.

are also born biologically as both male and female. Known in the past as hermaphrodites, "intersex" is now the modern term used. When babies are born as intersex, the parents and doctor often immediately make a determination, and the child is raised according to that decision. But studies have found that some intersex children ultimately identify as a gender other than the one by which they were raised.

"Even with evidence of many sexes, we continue to insist on just two," said Erickson-Schroth. "Until recently, physicians attempted to erase intersex people by performing surgery on them in early child-

A drag queen is a male who dresses and makes himself up as a woman for the purposes of a performance.

hood and insisting that they choose a gender in order to fit in."

As for the other terms under the umbrella of being transgender, it can be challenging to understand all of them and know how they relate to one another. The

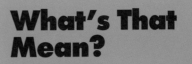
word "crossdresser" usually refers to a man who dresses as a woman, also known as a transvestite. Erickson-Schroth explained that although these terms can apply to women who dress as men, the term is rarely applied to women, "probably because we are more tolerant of women dressing in traditionally male clothing." She said that crossdressers often dress only in certain situations and do not live entirely as the opposite sex. Rather, many identify as straight men.

Drag queens are men who perform as women for entertainment purposes. Similarly, drag kings are women who perform as men.

"People who participate in drag often have exciting stage ***personas*** that exaggerate gender stereotypes," Erickson-Schroth explained. "These stage personalities are separate from their own gender identities, which are often in line with their assigned genders."

EXTRA INFO

Sometimes children, and even adolescents, like to dress in the clothing of the opposite sex. During puberty, a time of major change in an individual's body and life, it is not uncommon for questioning about gender to occur. This is a normal part of exploring identity.

Also, dissatisfaction with a culture's definition of gender role does not necessarily equal a transgender identity. Television shows from the 1950s and 1960s could give you the impression that women were only wives and mothers, teachers, and nurses. When a woman was shown participating in another career, she was often looked upon with suspicion. For many years, it was considered inappropriate for women to wear pants, and in some parts of society, it is still frowned on or even prohibited.

For the most part, cultural stereotypes about what is gender acceptable have fallen by the wayside. To make that happen, it was necessary for individuals to fight for change, bravely standing up to long-held beliefs and practices. The fact that these individuals—male and female—did not follow cultural norms for their sex does not mean they had any form of transgender issues. Their issues were with society and its restrictions.

In other words, a man who performs as a drag queen generally still lives as a man in his daily life, dressing like a man and filling a male gender role. In many cases, they are homosexual men. However, it is becoming more common for transgender people to also perform drag, though their characters on stage are still different from their day-to-day identities.

This illustrates the complicated ways in which gender identity differs from sexual orientation. Someone who is transgender isn't necessarily gay. And even the meaning of "gay" and "straight" can be confusing. A transman—born female but living as a man—who is attracted to women most often identifies as straight.

"It can be challenging to be in a relationship with a transgender person," said Barrett, who was involved in a long-term relationship with a transman. "Before we got together, I considered myself a lesbian. And he would get really upset about that, because even though he was still biologically a female, he identified as a guy. So according to him that made both of us straight, because we were a man and a woman in a relationship. At the end of the day, those are really just labels. But it made a difference, because the way other people see us really affects the way we see ourselves. So if people thought of us as a lesbian couple, then it took away from his identity or his feeling of being a man."

Considering all of the questions and the opportunities for confusion, many people are concerned about how to properly address someone who identifies as transgender. Dr. Erickson-Schroth gives some very simple advice in those situations.

"I encourage you to ask the people who you speak with how they identify," said Erickson-Schroth. "It is their opinion that matters, after all."

FIND OUT MORE ON THE INTERNET

Transgender Terminology
www.banyancounselingcenter.com/tsterminology.html

Transsexual Roadmap
www.tsroadmap.com/index.html

READ MORE ABOUT IT

Feinberg, Leslie. *Trans Liberation: Beyond Pink and Blue.* Boston, Mass.: Beacon Press, 1998.

Usher, Raven. *North American Lexicon of Transgender Terms.* San Francisco, Calif.: GLB Publishers, 2006.

chapter 3

Growing Up Transgender

When Armand was about two years old, his mother found him wearing an old Minnie Mouse dress. He refused to take it off.

"It was like, 'NO!'" she said. "Feet in a stance, a strong stance, just standing there. . . . She pretty much from that point on slept in it, stayed in it all day."

In 2008, National Public Radio featured a story on Armand and his family. To respect the family's privacy, they did not reveal their last name. But the family spoke openly about how Armand struggled with gender identity.

Though he was born male, by the time the piece aired several years later, both parents referred to Armand as "she." Although they tried to convince Armand to wear girls' clothing only in the house, out of fear for what neighbors would say, Armand's will was too strong. There were frequent tantrums, outbursts, and general unhappiness. Armand's parents sought medical advice and were given all sorts of diagnoses and treatments—but nothing worked.

Finally they found a psychologist who identified that Armand had Gender Identity Disorder, the term used for individuals who believe they have been born into the wrong biological body. Though his parents were relieved to understand what was happening, and agreed to stop trying to force Armand to live as a boy, they had another concern. By that time Armand was eleven years old, and getting close to puberty.

"We knew that puberty was around the corner and we needed to start looking into (what to do)," Armand's father said. "How do we help this child . . . develop in a way that is consistent with who she is?"

If sexual maturity and the development of secondary sex characteristics are postponed, males and females become nearly indistinguishable.

Then they learned about a radical treatment that had been used in similar situations to postpone puberty. This involved injections that would block hormones from being released in the body, stopping sexual maturity.

"If you can block the gonads, that is the ovary or the testis, from making its sex steroids, that being estrogen or testosterone, then you can literally prevent . . . almost all the physical differences between the genders," said Norman Spack, an *endocrinologist* at Children's Hospital in Boston, who was one of the first physicians to use this treatment in the United States. He noted that the process results in the patients being infertile, due to damage done to the gonads.

What's That Mean?

An *endocrinologist* is a medical doctor who specializes in the treatment of hormonal diseases and disorders.

In the second stage of the treatment, which would occur around age sixteen, the person can then choose to begin maturing sexually into the opposite gender by taking hormones of the opposite sex.

"We can make it possible that they can fit in, in the way they want to," Spack said. "It is really quite amazing."

This is remarkably different from the difficulty and trauma of trying to fit in as a transgender adult, especially for men who develop male attributes such as height, an Adam's apple, large hands and feet, and other physical characteristics that are difficult to change when transitioning to a female as an adult. Armand immediately chose this course of action and began living full time as a girl named Violet. On her first day at school as a female, Violet nervously followed her parents into the school building.

"We said, 'No! You are not going to do this. You're not going to walk behind anybody,'" Her father said. "'We're going to walk together.' And we held hands and we marched right up the sidewalk into those doors."

Although Violet's school was supportive, they were afraid of teasing or violence from other classmates. Nothing happened. The family said that after making the decision to allow Violet to transition, their lives became much happier and simpler.

But not everyone agrees that this is the best course of action. Adolescence is a very confusing time for young people, and making the decision to transition can have a significant and lasting effect on their lives.

"You can have a child who is presenting with absolute certainty, but it may be that at a later point they will decide that is not in fact what they want and their feelings may indeed change," said Polly Carmichael, a British psychologist who works at the Portman Clinic in London. Young people enrolled in treatment

All of us have both masculine and feminine aspects of our personality, no matter what our sexual identity is. This becomes a problem for people, however, when these aspects are so strongly out of sync with their biological sex that they are unable to feel that their own bodies express their gender identities.

at that clinic were required to live as the gender they were born, and more than 80 percent opted to stay that sex in adulthood. However, researchers in the Netherlands, where the treatment was developed, found that all the young people who chose to participate in their study remained the opposite gender into adulthood.

Meg Clark has an eleven-year-old daughter who is transgender. During a time when many schoolchildren learn about sexuality and physical development, Clark noted that there were very limited resources for the information her daughter needed to help her development.

Transgender issues are not unique to the modern Western world. In the past, in Asian cultures, however, being transgender was accepted and often even respected.

"Her whole class is separated by male and female on a special day to go to 'learning about your bodies,'" Clark said. "She's so sad she has none to go to."

Clark, like Violet's parents, accepted that her child was dealing with issues of sexual identity. But it's more likely that parents are confused by gender-variant children and try to force them to fit into traditional gender roles. This is often because parents don't understand that there are alternatives. And they know that other people may subject children who are different from their peers to teasing, harassment, and even violence.

"Being a parent of a gender-variant child can be really hard," said Dr. Laura Erickson-Schroth. "Most parents want to be understanding of their children, but they recognize that the world can be an unkind and even dangerous place for those who don't conform."

In 2010, Erickson-Schroth edited the book *Trans Bodies, Trans Selves*, a book written by and for gender-variant people, specifically created for adolescents and young adults with questions about their gender identity.

"I'd especially love for adolescents to read the section on transgender history, because all too often generations of people are cut off from each other and prevented from coming together around common social and political goals," said Erickson-Schroth.

Forcing children to live according to standard gender roles will not change how they personally indentify. And for young people who recognize that they are gender variant, they may suffer depression, anxiety, and even suicidal thoughts when they are expected to deny their personal identity.

This is why education and understanding is so important. When someone identifies as a specific gender, it is most helpful to them to respect their personal identity. Friends and family members of gender-variant young people are often unsure how to proceed or what is expected of them. The most important thing is to listen and maintain an open mind.

As Violet's sister learned, being transgender often means feeling as if you are living in the wrong body. That can be frightening, confusing, and disturbing.

"To go through the process of the gender that you're really not . . . that must be the most scariest, most disgusting thing," said Violet's sister, Melina. "I can't even imagine what that's like."

There are numerous organizations available to provide support for transgender youth and their families. TransYouth Family Allies has an online support group for parents called TYFA Talk and provides information for schools and health-care providers. TransFamily has an e-mail discussion group for parents as well as children and teens. The group

I'm a kid
I live next door

I'm in your class
I go to your church

I might even be *your* kid...

and I am
TRANSGENDER

MANY YOUTH DO NOT EXPRESS OR EXPERIENCE THEIR GENDER IN A WAY THAT MEETS SOCIAL OR FAMILY EXPECTATIONS. 1 OF 250 ARE TRANSGENDER.

SOMETIMES, A BOY IDENTIFIES AS A GIRL OR A GIRL IDENTIFIES AS A BOY. IT'S OK.

THEY ARE SIMPLY BEING THEMSELVES.

For more information visit:
www.TransActiveOnline.org

TransActive™
Supporting children & youth of all genders

TransActive Education & Advocacy is a non-profit organization

TransActive is one of the organizations that works as an advocate for transgender children.

Gender Spectrum's website provides many health and human services resources, and even hosts events and support groups.

Violet's father, who has spent many years coming to accept his new daughter, now gets offended by people who think she was incapable of understanding her gender at such a young age.

"(They) say, 'Well, she's too young to know!' Well, when did you know you were a girl? When did I know I was a boy?" he said. "I knew my whole life. I can't tell you exactly when, but it wasn't like I was ten and realized, 'Oh gee, I must be a boy!' What people fail to realize is they made that decision way earlier than that. It just happened that their gender identity and their anatomy matched."

FIND OUT MORE ON THE INTERNET

Gender Identity Disorder
www.webmd.com/sex/gender-identity-disorder

Links for Transgender Youth, Parents, and Social Services Providers
www.genderadvocates.org/Tyra/TYRALinks.html

Trans Youth Family Allies
imatyfa.org/

READ MORE ABOUT IT

Driver, Susan. *Queer Youth Cultures.* Albany, N.Y.: State University of New York Press, 2008.

Winfield, Cynthia L. *Gender Identity: The Ultimate Teen Guide.* Lanham, Md.: Scarecrow Press, 2007.

chapter 4

Living as a Transgender Adult

Most people don't realize how much gender identity factors into their lives. But every day, people make decisions and take actions based on their gender. So for transgender adults, this means many considerations and adjustments.

"It's interesting because, when you really stop to think about it, gender is everywhere—using the restroom, shopping for clothing, even having casual conversations," said Helena Barrett, who assists transgender adults to find health and human services. "Workplace dynamics can be challenging under ordinary circumstances. But for transgender people, it can be very complicated and even difficult, especially if people don't understand what it means or are ignorant about gender issues."

What's That Mean?

Advocacy is the process of sticking up for a group of people, speaking out on their behalf.

The Human Rights Campaign is the nation's largest lesbian, gay, bisexual, and transgender **advocacy** group. According to their research, employees who are transitioning—in other words, going from biologically female to male or male to female—may encounter conflicts with cultural standards. Colleagues who know they are transitioning may expect them to continue to act as their birth gender, even if it no longer applies to them. Even worse, people could lose their jobs because of their transitioning status. In most states, there are no laws prohibiting people from being fired because of their gender identity.

The LGBT flag represents and affirms the identity of lesbians, gays, bisexuals, and transgender people.

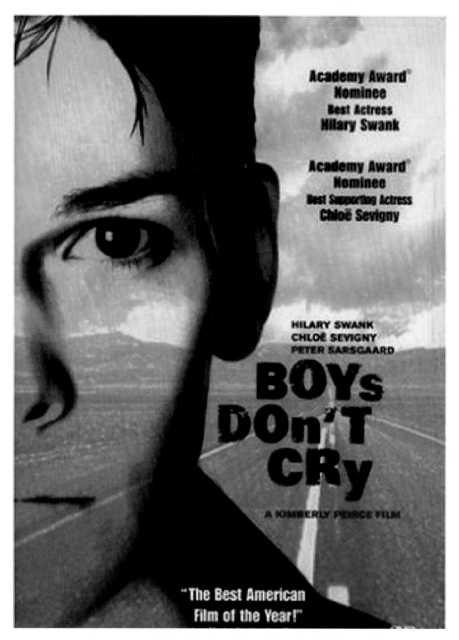

Boys Don't Cry *received overwhelmingly positive acclaim from critics. Lead actress Swank was awarded the 1999 Academy Award for Best Actress for her role in the movie.*

"As a minister, a counselor, and an advocate for transgender people, I have known far too many, and have heard far too many more stories of, men and women in dire situations because they cannot find or keep a job—not because they are unqualified, lazy, or incompetent—but simply because they have the courage to be who they truly are," Presbyterian minister Reverend Erin Swenson said in testimony for a congressional hearing on workplace discrimination against transgender people in 2008. "As a transgender woman, I experienced this discrimination first hand, when my transition from male to female threatened my ability to continue my role as an ordained minister in the Presbyterian Church. It is my sincere hope that, by learning from stories like mine through this hearing, Congress can move toward protecting transgender people from discrimination."

Tragically, this protection will come too late for some people, including Teena Brandon.

In 1999, actress Hilary Swank won an Academy Award for *Boys Don't Cry* and her portrayal of Teena Brandon and Brandon Teena in a story that showed how cruel individuals can be.

Teena Brandon was born in Lincoln, Nebraska, in 1972. Although born female, Teena considered herself to be male for much of her life. When she was in high school, Teena would stuff rolled socks in the front of her pants, bind her breasts, call herself Billy, and date girls from other schools. She even got engaged to two girls. Teena didn't keep her masquerade a secret from everyone. Her mother knew that Teena believed she was a male, and Teena told some of her friends. But the more people she told, the more difficult things got for her.

Teena was not a model of good behavior. She became adept at lying, she stole, and she forged checks. Her criminal behavior made a bad situation worse, and in 1993, she decided to start a new life in a new town with a new identity—Brandon Teena.

Life for Brandon in the small Nebraska town of Humboldt seemed to be going well. People accepted Brandon, and he made many friends, male and female. He even fell in love. But though Brandon changed his location and his identity, he fell into Teena's old habits when he ran out of money. His forgery landed him in jail in December 1993, and his sex put him in the female section of the jail.

Brandon's stint in the Humboldt jail blew his cover as a male, especially when he was listed as being female in the town newspaper's story about his arrest. His girlfriend, Lana, confronted him, and Brandon told her that he was saving money to undergo sex reassignment surgery.

On Christmas Eve, Brandon and Lana attended a party with friends, including Tom Nissen and John

Lotter. Nissen and Lotter decided to prove to Lana that Brandon was female, and prove to Brandon that "his kind" shouldn't be involved with Lana. After Lana left the party, Nissen beat and kicked Brandon. Afterward, Nissen and Lotter drove Brandon to a secluded area, where each raped him and then left him, coatless in the cold.

Although Nissen and Lotter had warned Brandon not to tell anyone of the attack, Lana convinced him to go to the hospital and call the sheriff. Sheriff Charles Laux took Brandon's statement, but his questions were directed more toward Brandon's lifestyle than the rape and assault. Reports indicate that the sheriff even referred to Brandon as "it." He questioned Brandon about his sexual experiences—including whether or not he was a virgin. Clearly, Sheriff Laux did not take Brandon's claims seriously.

A few days after Brandon signed a complaint against Nissen and Lotter, deputy sheriffs questioned the suspects and prepared to arrest them. However, Sheriff Laux would not authorize the arrest to take place, so they remained free.

Their freedom cost Brandon Teena his life. On December 30, Nissen and Lotter found Brandon at the home of Lisa Lambert. The pair murdered Teena, along with Lambert and a friend of Lambert's. Lambert's baby son was left alone in the house with the bodies.

Nissen and Lotter were immediate suspects, and they were arrested the following afternoon. Both were convicted of the murders.

Sheriff Laux's lack of action in Brandon's rape and assault disgusted many, including Brandon's mother, JoAnn Brandon. She filed a wrongful death suit against the sheriff, claiming that his mishandling of the rape and assault charges led to Brandon's death. Laux claimed he was trying to avoid a rush to judgment that might compromise any upcoming case. Although a lower Nebraska court dismissed the suit, the Nebraska Supreme Court reinstated it, because the sheriff had told Nissen and Lotter about the complaint but had not offered Brandon protection.

Brandon Teena's life was short and tragic because of transgender prejudice.

The lower court found in favor of Brandon's mother and awarded her approximately $17,000. Again, the Nebraska Supreme Court stepped in, ruling that the amount was too little and ordered that it be increased.

This tragic case—and the movie that was based on it—brought this issue out into the light. Organizations and governments around the world are taking steps to include protections for transgender people. Many companies now have policies that do not allow discrimination based on sexual orientation or gender identity. Some group insurance policies include health coverage for medical procedures relating to transitioning, and the Human Rights Campaign provides information to assist transgender employees and their companies.

As part of the 2008 congressional hearing, the Business Coalition for Workplace Fairness submitted a letter or support that said, in part:

> To make our workplace values clear and transparent to our employees, customers and investors, each of our businesses have already implemented a non-discrimination policy, which is inclusive of gender identity and/or gender expression. This policy has been accepted broadly and we believe it has positively affected our bottom-line. Our philosophy and practice of valuing diversity encourages full and open

participation by all employees. By treating all employees with fairness and respect we have been able to recruit and retain the best and brightest workers, thereby bringing a multitude of diverse opinions and perspectives to our organizations.

The statement was signed by dozens of supporting businesses that included Bank of America, Microsoft Corporation, General Motors Corporation, Eastman Kodak, Levi Strauss & Company, and Google Inc.

Workplace issues of discrimination often come from confusion about what it means to be transgender. The American Psychiatric Association (APA) still includes "gender identity disorder" in its *Diagnostic and Statistical Manual of Mental Disorders* (DSM), which leads some people to think that being transgender is a mental problem. Some individuals then become concerned for their safety if they have transgender co-workers.

"In my opinion, gender-variance is not a mental illness, but is instead a normal variation," said Dr.

Laura Erickson-Schroth, a mental-health worker. "We sometimes forget that just because something is less common, that does not mean that it is abnormal or unhealthy. Our ideas about gender norms and roles make it very easy for us to jump to the conclusion that those who don't fit our *stereotypes* are mentally ill, but that is only because it is easier than challenging our own assumptions about gender. Long before we are born, the world is preparing for our entrance in blue or pink."

According to Erickson-Schroth, "Individuals who identify as transgender are classified as having gender identity disorder (GID) in the . . . DSM, which mental health providers use to diagnose mental illness."

The DSM, which is due for another revision in 2013, may be altered to change this diagnosis, which has been very *controversial.* However, there are important reasons for maintaining GID as a recognized medical condition.

"One of the reasons for retaining the GID diagnosis in some form in the DSM is that many people use the diagnosis to receive psychological services and medical care, such as hormones and surgery," Erickson-Schroth said. "In the medical field, diagnostic codes are very important for billing. In order to be reimbursed for assessment or treatment, health-care providers must write down the suspected diagnosis along with its code."

Lambda Legal has been outspoken on behalf of trangender rights.

In 2010, the APA's recommendations for changes to the DSM were made available for public review.

"Upon reviewing the APA's proposed revisions, it appears that they no longer consider gender identity that differs from birth sex to be a basis for psychiatric diagnosis," said Human Rights Campaign Associate Director of Diversity Allyson Robinson. "By focusing instead on the experience of *incongruence*, an often distressing conflict between a person's physical characteristics and their sense of gender identity, the APA has made an important step toward the *destigmatization* of transgender lives."

A survey by Lambda Legal, an LGBT advocacy organization, found that 70 percent of transgender respondents experienced discrimination by health-care providers. Erickson-Schroth notes that some commonplace adjustments can be made to make environments more trans-friendly, such as having gender-neutral bathrooms, and including "transgender" as an option on official forms, such as medical intake forms. This can make it easier for patients

What's That Mean?

Incongruence is a feeling of inner conflict over parts of a person's identity that don't fit together, for example biological gender and gender identity.

Destigmatization is the process of getting over feelings of shame and rejection that have been associated with certain behaviors or groups of people.

EXTRA INFO

Some people don't identify either as male or female, which can cause problems when deciding which pronouns to use. If someone doesn't feel like a man or a woman, neither "he" nor "she" really describes who they are. Because English doesn't have any non-gendered pronouns, the genderqueer community has developed its own gender-neutral words. Many genderqueer individuals choose to go by the pronouns ze/zir/zirs (instead of he/him/his or she/her/hers), and this is probably the most popular alternative. Other gender-neutral pronouns that have been suggested include thon/thons/thons, ve/ver/vis, and en/ens/ens.

to address the topic with their doctors. Similarly, she suggests allowing space for a preferred name, in the event a transperson prefers to be known as something other than his or her birth name.

"*Cultural competence* is an issue in health care for many communities—sexual minorities, different racial or ethnic groups, those with disabilities, incarcerated people—the list goes on. For future physicians, medical school should be a place where these issues are discussed and taught. Currently, medical schools do a poor job preparing students for the health issues of lesbian, gay, bisexual, and transgender people."

Despite these challenges, though, significant improvements have been made in achieving equality for transgender people. In June 2010, the U.S. State Department announced changes in policy guidelines regarding gender change on passports and other documents used by U.S. citizens when traveling abroad. The policy states that the gender listed on passports can be changed when documentation is provided from a medical doctor stating that the individual has undergone appropriate medical treatment for gender transition.

"We are grateful to the State Department for taking the necessary steps towards securing respectful treatment of transgender people who deserve to travel safely," said Dru Levasseur, Transgender Rights Attorney for Lambda Legal. "When traveling at home and abroad, transgender people have been subject to dangerous situations because their passports did not reflect their gender. These new guidelines will make travel safer for transgender people."

What's That Mean?

Cultural competence is the ability to communicate effectively and get along with people from different backgrounds.

Amanda Simpson was the first openly transgender presidential appointee.

High-profile transgender people have also brought greater public understanding of gender issues. In 2010, Amanda Simpson began her role in the United States Commerce Department. Simpson, the country's first openly transgender presidential appointee, began her transition in 2000. As a former test pilot, she worked in aerospace and defense for about three decades. President Barack Obama appointed her to a role related to the licensing and enforcement for exports of military technology.

"Being the first sucks," she said about her new position. "I'd rather not be the first but someone has to be. . . . I'm experienced and very well qualified to deal with anything that might show up because I've broken barriers at lots of other places and I always win people over with who I am and what I can do."

Throughout the 1990s, Chastity Bono, the daughter of cultural icon Cher and singer-turned-politician Sonny Bono, was an outspoken advocate for lesbian, gay, bisexual, and transgender rights. In 2009, Bono announced transitioning from female to male, using the name Chaz.

"This announcement by Chaz is nothing short of courageous," said Human Rights Campaign president Joe Solmonese.

His decision to be public about his transition speaks to the courage he has in living his life openly and honestly, and will also undoubtedly help foster much-needed dialogue about the lives of transgender Americans and the need for full equality.

It is our hope that all of us can feel great pride that we live in a country where each one of us has the ability to be true to our own identity. From the time we are born, we are taught that there are girls and there are boys. But like our history, our communities are rich with people who have blurred, blended, or crossed

Chaz Bono's openly transgender identity has helped bring acceptance and awareness to trangender issues. He is shown here with his partner Jennifer Elia.

those lines. Chaz is now part of an impressive and remarkable group of Americans who have made our country a better place simply by being true to themselves.

FIND OUT MORE ON THE INTERNET

Human Rights Campaign
www.hrc.org/

The Official Chaz Bono Website
chazbono.net/

Transgender Resources
www.gendertalk.com/info/resource/index.shtml

READ MORE ABOUT IT

Currah, Paisley, Richard Juang, and Shannon Miner. *Transgender Rights.* Minneapolis, Minn.: University of Minnesota Press, 2006.

Girshick, Lori B. *Transgender Voices: Beyond Women and Men.* Lebanon, N.H.: University Press of New England, 2008.

BIBLIOGRAPHY

Erickson-Schroth, Laura. "Answers About Transgender Issues." *The New York Times*, April 22, 2010.

Gender Spectrum, www.genderspectrum.org (8 June 2010).

Goldman, Russell. "First Transgender Presidential Appointee Fears Being Labeled 'Token.'" *ABC News,* January 5, 2010.

Human Rights Campaign, www.hrc.org (8 June 2010).

Lambda Legal, www.lambdalegal.com (7 June 2010).

Lewis-Davis, Brittany. "Stepping Outside Gender Roles Affects Men and Women Differently." *Mental Health News,* June 19, 2010.

Opie, Iona and Peter Opie. *The Oxford Dictionary of Nursery Rhymes*. New York: Oxford University Press, 1997.

Spiegel, Alix. "Parents Consider Treatment to Delay Son's Puberty." National Public Radio, May 8, 2008.

TransYouth Family Allies, www.imatyfa.org (6 June 2010).

U.S. Department of State, www.state.gov (6 June 2010).

INDEX

ABOUT THE AUTHOR AND THE CONSULTANT

Jaime A. Seba's involvement in LGBT issues began in 2004, when she helped open the doors of the Pride Center of Western New York, which served a community of more than 100,000 people. As head of public education and outreach, she spearheaded one of the East Coast's first crystal methamphetamine awareness and harm reduction campaigns. She also wrote and developed successful grant programs through the Susan G. Komen Breast Cancer Foundation, securing funding for the region's first breast cancer prevention program designed specifically for gay, bisexual, and transgender women. Jaime studied political science at Syracuse University before switching her focus to communications with a journalism internship at the Press & Sun-Bulletin in Binghamton, New York, in 1999. She is currently a freelance writer based in Seattle.

James T. Sears specializes in research in lesbian, gay, bisexual, and transgender issues in education, curriculum studies, and queer history. His scholarship has appeared in a variety of peer-reviewed journals and he is the author or editor of twenty books and is the Editor of the *Journal of LGBT Youth*. Dr. Sears has taught curriculum, research, and LGBT-themed courses in the departments of education, sociology, women's studies, and the honors college at several universities, including: Trinity University, Indiana University, Harvard University, Penn State University, the College of Charleston, and the University of South Carolina. He has also been a Research Fellow at Center for Feminist Studies at the University of Southern California, a Fulbright Senior Research Southeast Asia Scholar on sexuality and culture, a Research Fellow at the University of Queensland, a consultant for the J. Paul Getty Center for Education and the Arts, and a Visiting Research Lecturer in Brazil. He lectures throughout the world.